Building the Temple

The York Rite and Its Influence on Freemasonry

William Kennedy

The York Rite and Its Influence on Freemasonry

DEDICATION

CONTENTS

The Origins of the York Rite

From Operative to Speculative Freemasonry

Stonemasons' craft guilds in the middle ages are where the traditions that would later become known as the York Rite may be found. These guilds were responsible for the construction of a large number of the great cathedrals and other notable buildings throughout Europe, such as Notre Dame de Paris, Westminster Abbey, and the Cologne Cathedral. Other examples include the creation of other significant buildings. The members of these guilds were highly skilled artisans who were organized into lodges, sometimes known as chapters. Each lodge or chapter had its own master and wardens to oversee the activities within the lodge.

The construction of the Temple of Solomon, which was thought to be one of the most important aspects of the craft, was the impetus behind the organization of the lodges that comprised operative Freemasonry. The individuals who were a part of these lodges may attain one of three degrees: apprentice, fellowcraft, or master mason. The job of apprentice was considered an entry-level post since it required acquiring the fundamental abilities of the craft, whereas the position of fellowcraft was considered an intermediate position because it required more advanced training. It was the responsibility of the master mason, who held the highest degree in the trade, to oversee the work of the apprentices and fellowcrafts.

During the 17th and 18th centuries, a new type of Freemasonry that came to be known as speculative Freemasonry evolved in response to the gradual downfall of the guilds. Those who were interested in the symbolism and theory of the craft made comprised the members of the theoretical lodges, in contrast to the operative lodges, which were made up of actual stonemasons working in the trade. Instead of focusing on constructing a physical replica of the Temple of Solomon, Speculative Freemasonry was organized on the concept of constructing the spiritual Temple of the Soul.

Around this historical period, the York Rite started to take form and become more organized. The second major branch of Freemasonry is called the Scottish Rite, while the York Rite is one of the two major branches of Freemasonry. The city of York in England, which was a prominent hub for the craft during the Middle Ages, is where the practice first began, which is why it is known by that name today. Chapter, Council, and Commandery are the three principal groups that make up the York Rite. The York Rite was founded in 1738.

The administration of four different degrees, namely the Royal Arch, the Most Excellent Master, the Mark Master, and the Past Master, is the responsibility of the Chapter. These degrees are concerned with the reconstruction of the Temple of Solomon as well as the recovery of the Word that was misplaced. The Mark Master degree focuses on the marking of stones by the artisans, whilst the Past Master degree focuses on the historical and symbolic components of the craft. Both degrees are awarded to those who demonstrate excellence in their respective fields. The Most Excellent Master degree focuses on completing the Temple, whereas the Royal Arch degree concentrates on finding the lost Word. Both degrees are part of the Freemasonry organization.

The Council is in charge of the administration of three degrees, namely the Royal Master, Select Master, and Super Excellent Master degrees. These degrees are in the order of increasing difficulty. These degrees focus on the uncovering of King Solomon's hidden treasury as well as the maintenance of the craft. The construction of the hidden vault is the focus of the Royal Master degree, whereas the uncovering of the vault is the focus of the Select Master degree. The subject of study for the Super Excellent Master degree is the maintenance of the craft and the onward transmission of its teachings.

The Commandery is responsible for the administration of three degrees, known as the Order of the Red Cross, the Order of Malta, and the Order of the Temple. The history and legend of the Knights Templar, who were an influential military organization during the Middle Ages, are the focus of these degrees. The degree of the Order of the Red Cross focuses on the life of the Knight before he became a Templar, whereas the degree of the Order of Malta focuses on the life of the Knight after he became a Templar. The Order of the Temple degree is focused with the history and legend of the Knights Templar and their quest for the Holy Grail.

The York Rite may be traced back to the late 18th century, when a group of Freemasons in New York made the decision to establish a new Grand Lodge that would be dedicated to the York Rite. This event is considered to be the starting point of the York Rite. This new Grand Lodge was formed in 1797 and it immediately acquired popularity among Freemasons in the United States. Throughout the course of the 19th century, the York Rite maintained its rapid growth and expansion, and by the beginning of the 20th century, it had established itself as one of the most influential Masonic orders in the United States.

There are thousands of lodges and chapters dedicated to practicing the York Rite in nations all over the world, including the

United States of America, Canada, England, Scotland, and Australia, to name a few. The York Rite is a branch of Freemasonry that is well-known for its concentration on the historical and traditional parts of the fraternity in addition to its emphasis on the symbolic and allegorical aspects of the craft.

The Degrees of the York Rite
A Comprehensive Overview

The Royal Arch Chapter, the Cryptic Council, and the Commandery of Knights Templar are the three principal bodies that make up the York Rite. Each of these organizations offers a series of degrees, sometimes known as stages of initiation, to its members. These degrees are intended to provide the initiate with specific knowledge and instruction. In the following chapter, we shall present an all-encompassing summary of the degrees that are awarded by the York Rite.

The Royal Arch Chapter is the first body of the York Rite and is composed of the four degrees of the York Rite: the Mark Master, the Past Master, the Most Excellent Master, and the Royal Arch. The studies for the Mark Master degree center on the construction of the Temple of King Solomon and the part that stonemasons played in that process. The significance of the cornerstone in the construction process and the significance of the mark that is set on it are both investigated as part of the degree program. The applicant for the degree of Past Master learns about the history and traditions of the Masonic lodge, as well as receiving training on how to rule and manage a lodge as part of their education for this degree. The candidate for the Most Excellent Master degree learns about the significance of spiritual construction while delving into the symbolism and allegory of the Temple of Solomon. The final degree, which is the Royal Arch degree, is the conclusion of the Royal Arch Chapter. It exposes the lost word of a Master Mason, which was lost when the Temple of Solomon was destroyed.

The second group that makes up the York Rite is called the Cryptic Council, and it is made up of three degrees: the Royal Master, the Select Master, and the Super Excellent Master. The Royal Master degree focuses on the myth of the buried riches that was misplaced after the Temple of Solomon was destroyed, as well as the search for that treasure. The candidate for the Select Master degree learns about the significance of conserving sacred knowledge as well as the history and symbolism of the crypt in the Temple of Solomon as part of their coursework for the degree. The topic of the destruction of the Temple of Solomon and the dispersion of the Jewish people is discussed in the Super Excellent Master degree, which is widely regarded as the most esoteric degree offered by the York Rite.

The Order of the Temple, the Order of the Red Cross, and the Order of Malta are the three degrees that make up the ultimate body of the York Rite, which is known as the Commandery of Knights Templar. The narrative of the Jewish people's captivity in Babylonia and the part that the prophet Zerubbabel played in facilitating their return to Jerusalem is at the center of the Order of the Red Cross. Candidates for membership in the Order of Malta get instruction on the chivalric traditions of the Knights of Malta as well as the significance of acts of charity and hospitality. The York Rite eventually leads up to the Order of the Temple, which investigates the history and legend of the Knights Templar. This is the final step in the process. Candidates for the degree learn about the valor and devotion of the Knights Templar, as well as their determination to uphold and defend the Christian faith.

In Freemasonry, the degrees of the York Rite offer a thorough education on the history, symbolism, and allegory of the fraternity's various degrees. Initiates progress through a series of degrees, each of which is intended to teach them a specific lesson or collection of teachings that will assist them in developing a deeper comprehension of the spiritual principles upon which the craft is founded. Freemasons have the opportunity to expand their knowledge of their trade and to forge closer ties to the organization's past, as well as its traditions and customs, by working through the various degrees of the York Rite.

The Royal Arch Degree

The Foundation of the York Rite

As the degree that serves as the foundation for the York Rite, the Royal Arch degree is often regarded as being among the most prestigious and consequential degrees in all of Freemasonry. This degree is frequently referred to as the "completion" of the Master Mason degree, and it discloses the word of a Master Mason that was lost at the fall of the Temple of Solomon. Also, this degree is often regarded as "completing" the Master Mason degree.

The narrative of King Solomon's Temple being reconstructed serves as the organizing principle for the degree. The candidate for the degree takes on the persona of a "Companion" who is assisting in the process of rebuilding the Temple. The underground vault in the remains of the Temple is where the story begins, and inside it are a variety of significant items, such as the Ark of the Covenant and the word that was forgotten by a Master Mason.

The candidate is then taken through a series of metaphorical and symbolic experiences that are intended to educate him on the significance of the Temple of Solomon and the significance of spiritual building. He is instructed on the significance of the cornerstone, and how it serves as a representation of the Temple's underlying structure. In addition to this, he is instructed on the meaning behind the pillars of Jachin and Boaz, which stand for the harmony that can be achieved when power and beauty coexist.

The most exciting part of the degree occurs when the candidate is taken into the Holy of Holies and given the task of finding the word of a Master Mason that has been lost. The message is communicated to him by the High Priest, and after that, he is elevated to the exalted degree of Royal Arch Mason.

It is common practice to view the Royal Arch degree as the completion of the first three degrees of Freemasonry. Moreover, the Royal Arch degree is regarded as an essential component of the Master Mason degree. It is also viewed as an important step in the spiritual path of a Freemason, since it teaches the candidate about the significance of spiritual building and the symbolism of the Temple of Solomon. This is seen as an important stage in the spiritual journey of a Freemason.

The Royal Arch degree is important not only because of its spiritual meaning, but also because of its historical relevance and its symbolic significance. It gives the candidate with a greater grasp of the symbolism and allegory that underpin the craft, in addition to teaching him about the history and traditions of Freemasonry. It also establishes a link between the candidate and the lengthy line of Masonic heritage as well as the numerous generations of Masons who have come before him in the fraternity.

It is widely acknowledged that the Royal Arch degree, which serves as the cornerstone of the York Rite, is among the most prestigious and significant degrees in all of Freemasonry. The candidate is educated on the significance of spiritual building as well as the symbolism of the Temple of Solomon, and the secret word of a Master Mason is made known. The degree is an important milestone on the spiritual path of a Freemason, and it links the aspirant with the extensive Masonic tradition that has come before them.

The Cryptic Degrees

Unlocking the Mysteries of Freemasonry

There is a series of Masonic degrees known as the Cryptic Degrees, and they are all a part of the York Rite. Due to the fact that they are not often recognized outside of the Masonic community, these degrees are frequently referred to using the terms "hidden" or "secret." There are three levels of mastery within the Cryptic Degrees: the Royal Master, the Select Master, and the Super Excellent Master.

The legend of King Solomon's Temple and its building serves as the inspiration for the Royal Master degree. It tells the narrative of how a secret vault was built beneath the Temple so that the Temple's riches might be stored there. The vault was utilized to keep the treasures. The aspirant receives instruction on the need of maintaining confidentiality and discretion, as well as the perils of divulging Masonic trade secrets.

The legend of the fall of the temple built by King Solomon serves as the inspiration for the Select Master degree. It narrates the narrative of a group of Masons who managed to flee the Temple before to its demolition and make their way to the city of Tyre. During their journey, they encountered many trials and tribulations along the way. The candidate is instructed on the significance of maintaining a positive attitude and remaining resilient in the face of challenges, as well as the value of brotherhood and providing support to one another.

The narrative of the Jewish people's enslavement in Babylonia provides the foundation for the Super Excellent Master degree. It narrates the account of a group of Freemasons who were enslaved by the Babylonians and compelled to serve in the court of King Nebuchadnezzar. These Freemasons were taken captive by the Babylonians. The candidate is instructed on the virtues of having faith and loyalty, as well as the benefits that come from serving a higher purpose, as part of the selection process.

It is common practice to view the Cryptic Degrees as a continuation of the teachings that are imparted in the Royal Arch degree. These are intended to impart upon the applicant a more in-depth knowledge of the history and customs of Freemasonry, as well as instruct him on the significance of maintaining secrecy, persevering through difficult times, and having faith in one's beliefs.

In addition to the significance they hold symbolically, the Cryptic Degrees are also significant due to the role they have played throughout history. They give the candidate a more in-depth knowledge of the history and customs of the Jewish people, as well as the role that Masons performed in maintaining those traditions. In addition to this, they link the candidate to the lengthy line of Masonic heritage as well as the numerous generations of Masons who came before him.

There is a sequence of Masonic degrees known as the Cryptic Degrees, and they are all a part of the York Rite. They come in three different levels: Royal Master, Select Master, and Very Excellent Master. The Royal Master is the highest level. These are intended to impart upon the applicant a more in-depth knowledge of the history and customs of Freemasonry, as well as instruct him on the significance of maintaining secrecy, persevering through difficult times, and having faith in one's beliefs. They are also significant due to their historical significance, as they link the candidate to the long line of Masonic tradition as well as the numerous generations of Masons who have come before him. This makes them valuable on multiple levels.

The Knights Templar Degree

History, Myth, and Legend

The Knights Templar Degree is often considered to be one of the most enigmatic and contentious degrees in the entirety of Freemasonry. It is considered by many to be the culmination of one's Masonic journey, and it is included in the York Rite. The mythology of the Knights Templar, a historical order of warrior-monks who were instrumental in the history of the Crusades, serves as the inspiration for this degree.

In the early 18th century, Masonic lodges in France started incorporating aspects of the Knights Templar mythology into their ritual, which is where the beginnings of the Knights Templar Degree can be traced back to. The Knights Templar Degree was named after this practice. These lodges came up with a new degree that they termed the "Order of the Temple." Its purpose was to pay homage to the memory of the Knights Templar and was given its name in their honor.

Masonic lodges in various regions of Europe quickly adopted the degree, and it finally made its way to lodges in the United States of America. In the United States, the degree was adopted by the York Rite and given the name "Knights Templar Degree." This occurred when the degree was brought to the country. It is currently one of the most well-known and widely practiced degrees in all of Freemasonry, making it one of the most popular degrees overall.

The Knights Templar Degree is a difficult and intricate degree that includes various aspects of history, mythology, and folklore into its coursework. It recounts the history of the Knights Templar and the part they played in the Crusades throughout that time period. In addition to this, it instructs the candidate on the significance of faith, virtue, and duty, and incorporates aspects of Christian symbolism and mythology in its design.

One of the most pervasive misconceptions concerning the Knights Templar Degree is the assumption that the order still operates incognito, and that its members are involved in an on-going search for wisdom and enlightenment. This myth has been kept alive by a number of well-known books and films that have presented the Knights Templar as a shadowy and enigmatic organization with ties to hidden organizations and occult traditions. These depictions have contributed to the perpetuation of the myth.

In point of fact, the Knights Templar were an actual historical order that was active from the 12th to the 14th century and operated between the years of 1200 and 1400. They were first established to safeguard pilgrims on their way to the Holy Land; however, they quickly became embroiled in military campaigns directed against the Muslims who resided in the Holy Land. Early in the 14th century, after gradually falling out of favor with both the church and the kingdom, the order was eventually dissolved.

In spite of the fact that they only existed for a brief period of time, the Knights Templar managed to leave an indelible mark on the collective consciousness and became the focus of a great number of myths and tales. Masons all around the world continue to be fascinated and inspired by the Knights Templar Degree, which maintains its status as one of the most well-known and intriguing degrees in the entirety of Freemasonry.

The Knights Templar Degree is a difficult and intricate degree that includes various aspects of history, mythology, and folklore into its coursework. It recounts the history of the Knights Templar and the part they played in the Crusades throughout that time period. In addition to this, it instructs the candidate on the significance of faith, virtue, and duty, and incorporates aspects of Christian symbolism and mythology in its design. In spite of its contentious past and pervasive falsehoods, the Knights Templar Degree continues to be an essential component of the Masonic legacy, and it continues to motivate and test Masons all over the world.

The Chivalric Orders of the York Rite

Knighthood in Freemasonry

There is a set of degrees within Freemasonry called the Chivalric Orders of the York Rite. These degrees are modeled after the traditions of knighthood during the middle ages. These degrees are referred to as the Order of the Red Cross, the Order of Malta, and the Order of the Temple (also known as the Knights Templar Degree), and many Masons believe that attaining one of these degrees represents the culmination of their Masonic journey.

When Masonic lodges in Europe started incorporating elements of medieval chivalry into their ritual, this is when the beginnings of the Chivalric Orders can be traced back to. The origins of the Chivalric Orders may be traced back to the early days of Freemasonry. These lodges came up with a brand new hierarchy of degrees in order to pay homage to the noble qualities associated with knights, such as bravery, honor, and loyalty.

These degrees eventually became more codified and were included into the York Rite throughout the course of time. Currently, these degrees are some of the most extensively performed and popular degrees in all of Freemasonry. They are also regarded by many as the pinnacle of Masonic ideas' ability to be expressed in written form.

The Order of the Red Cross is considered to be the first level of achievement within the Chivalric Orders. This degree is based on a story of a Christian knight who is attempting to reclaim the True Cross, which was taken by Muslims during the Crusades. The story takes place in an alternate reality. The candidate will learn the significance of maintaining their faith and tenacity in the face of challenges, as well as the value of actively seeking truth and enlightenment as part of the requirements for the degree.

The Order of Malta represents the second level of achievement within the Chivalric Orders. The history of the Knights Hospitaller, a medieval order of warrior-monks who gave medical attention to the sick and injured throughout the Crusades, serves as the foundation for this degree. The candidate is instructed on the significance of charity and compassion, and the degree places an emphasis on the Masonic principle of assisting people who are in need of assistance.

The Order of the Temple is the highest level that may be achieved in the Chivalric Orders (or Knights Templar Degree). The candidate is instructed on the significance of honor, responsibility, and self-sacrifice throughout the course of this degree, which is derived from the lore surrounding the Knights Templar. The degree is one of the most extensive and complicated in all of Freemasonry. It combines aspects of history, mythology, and the symbolism of Christianity.

Masons are taught about the values and virtues of knighthood, and they are inspired to live their lives in accordance with those ideals through participation in the Chivalric Orders of the York Rite. The Chivalric Orders of the York Rite are not just about historical reenactment or ritualistic performance. Masons are encouraged to use the principles of bravery, honor, loyalty, and self-sacrifice as a compass in their day-to-day lives as part of the degrees, which stress the significance of these characteristics.

There is a set of degrees within Freemasonry called the Chivalric Orders of the York Rite. These degrees are modeled after the traditions of knighthood during the middle ages. They are intended to celebrate the virtuous qualities of knights and to encourage Masons to model their own lives after those ideals as best they can. Masons are given a powerful and energizing picture of what it means to be a Masonic knight through the degrees, which are rich in symbolism, history, and mythology and provide Masons with a powerful and inspiring vision of what it means to be a Masonic knight.

The Scottish Rite and the York Rite

Similarities and Differences

The Scottish Rite and the York Rite are two of the most well-known and powerful rites that are associated with the fraternity of Freemasonry. Despite the fact that both of these divisions come from the same lineage and have many points in common, they are fundamentally diverse from one another in terms of their organizational makeup, degree structures, and philosophies.

Freemasonry's Scotch Rite is a sub-order that may be traced back to the 18th century in France, where it was first established. It is structured in 33 degrees, each of which is broken down further into one of three distinct sections: the Lodge of Perfection, the Council of Princes of Jerusalem, and the Consistory. The Scottish Rite degrees cover a broad spectrum of subjects, such as religion, philosophy, ethics, and morals, and they place an emphasis on the significance of an individual's own personal spiritual growth.

On the other hand, the York Rite is a subset of Freemasonry that was established in the United States in the 18th century. It is structured with the Royal Arch Chapter, the Cryptic Council, and the Knights Templar as its three primary governing organizations. In the York Rite degrees, the history and customs of medieval chivalry are studied, and the significance of moral and ethical concepts like charity, loyalty, and honor is emphasized. These are the three pillars around which the York Rite is built.

The degree structures of the Scottish Rite and the York Rite are very different from one another, which is one of the primary contrasts between the two orders. In comparison, the York Rite only has ten degrees, while the Scottish Rite has a total of 33. Yet, in contrast to the degrees of the Scottish Rite, which are more autonomous and diverse than their York Rite counterparts, the degrees of the York Rite are more closely tied to one another.

A further distinction that can be drawn between these two types of Freemasonry is how they are organized. The Scottish Rite is more centralized and hierarchical than other Masonic organizations, and it has a distinct chain of command and structure for its leadership. On the other side, the York Rite is characterized by a greater degree of decentralization and autonomy, with each body functioning independently of the others.

Both the Scottish Rite and the York Rite place a strong emphasis on the importance of moral and ethical standards, and they encourage its members to live their lives in accordance with these goals. This is a philosophical aspect shared by both orders. The York Rite, on the other hand, places a greater emphasis on the value of honor and duty, as well as the traditions of medieval chivalry and the growth of the individual's spirituality and intellect, whereas the Scottish Rite is more concerned with the growth of the individual.

Notwithstanding these distinctions, the Scottish Rite and the York Rite are both dedicated to the principles of Freemasonry and share a common heritage. Both of these organizations provide their members with opportunity for opportunities for personal growth and development, as well as a rich and satisfying experience. Whether they choose to join the Scottish Rite or the York Rite, Masons will discover a welcome and supportive community of persons who share their devotion to moral and ethical values, brotherhood, and charity. This community will exist regardless of whatever Rite the Mason decides to join.

The Influence of the York Rite on American Freemasonry

From the late 18th century, when American Freemasonry was first established, the York Rite has been an essential component in the growth and evolution of the organization. The York Rite has played a significant role in determining the path that American Freemasonry has taken and the nature of the organization as a whole, beginning with the establishment of the first Grand Encampment of Knights Templar in the United States and continuing with the founding of the General Grand Chapter of Royal Arch Masons.

The emphasis that the York Rite places on the traditions of medieval chivalry has been one of the most significant contributions that the York Rite has made to American Freemasonry. Among American Freemasons, the Knights Templar in particular have been a powerful force in the promotion of the values of honor, courage, and selflessness as ideals to strive for. The Templar degree has also served as a source of motivation for many American Masons. These Masons look to the Templars as an example of how to serve others and make sacrifices for the sake of society as a whole.

The York Rite has had a significant impact on American Freemasonry, one of the most important aspects of which has been the emphasis it places on the significance of the Royal Arch degree. Since the early days of the republic, the Royal Arch has been an important part of American Masonry. It has also been acknowledged as a necessary stage in the journey of a Mason who is seeking additional knowledge and enlightenment. From its founding in 1797 in the United States, the General Grand Chapter of Royal Arch Masons has been one of the most important organizations in terms of advancing the Royal

Arch degree and ensuring that it maintains its continuous life and relevance in today's society.

In addition to these specific contributions, the York Rite has been a driving force behind a significant number of broader trends and changes in American Freemasonry. These trends and developments include: For instance, the York Rite has been at the forefront of efforts to promote unity and cooperation among Masonic bodies, and it has worked to establish a framework for mutual recognition and cooperation among various Masonic jurisdictions. Other examples include the Scottish Rite, which has been at the forefront of efforts to promote unity and cooperation among Masonic bodies. The York Rite has also been a major proponent for the significance of ritual and symbolism in Freemasonry, and it has fought to ensure that these aspects continue to be at the center of the experience of becoming a Mason.

The position that the York Rite plays as a bridge between the realm of theoretical Masonry and the world of operative Masonry is another example of the influence that the York Rite has had on American Freemasonry. To connect modern-day Masons with the rich heritage of the operative Masons who built the cathedrals and castles of medieval Europe, the York Rite places a strong emphasis on the traditions of medieval chivalry and the symbolism of the building of King Solomon's Temple. This helps to bridge the gap between the two.

The York Rite has had a significant and far-reaching impact on American Freemasonry as a whole during the course of its history. From its commitment to the Royal Arch degree to its function as a bridge between the worlds of speculative and operative Masonry, the York Rite has played an important part in sculpting the personality and course of American Freemasonry for over two centuries. This can be seen in its emphasis on the values of medieval chivalry as well as its dedication to the degree of Royal Arch.

The York Rite and Its Connection to the Founding Fathers

Several of the individuals who are considered to be the "Founding Fathers" of the United States were members of the York Rite of Freemasonry. In point of fact, a number of the most influential people in the annals of American history were York Rite Masons, and the ties that link these two institutions are intricately linked.

George Washington, who is commonly considered to be one of the most prominent and influential members of the York Rite, is one of the Founding Fathers who had ties to the York Rite. This is one of the most notable connections between the York Rite and the Founding Fathers. In the year 1752, George Washington became a member of Freemasons, and he continued to be an active member of the fraternity throughout his whole life. As a member of the York Rite, George Washington was especially devoted to the Knights Templar degree. He saw this degree as a potent emblem of the virtues of chivalry and sacrifice that he aspired to embody in his own life and leadership, and he considered it as a powerful symbol of these values.

Benjamin Franklin, a key figure in American history, became a member of the York Rite in 1731 and was inducted into the fraternity at that time. Franklin was a staunch supporter of the principles upheld by Freemasonry, and he was of the opinion that the fraternity should play a significant part in advancing the ideas of individual liberty, civic virtue, and social peace that were at the core of the American Revolution.

John Hancock, Paul Revere, and Robert Livingston were among the other Founding Fathers who were also members of the York Rite. Their connections to the York Rite are a testament to the important role that Freemasonry played in the early years of the republic. Each of these individuals played an important role in the development of the United States, and their connections to the York Rite are a testament to the important role that Freemasonry played.

In addition to these specific links, the York Rite has also played a significant part in the larger cultural and political environment of the United States, making it one of the most influential organizations of its kind. Since the earliest days of American society, the York Rite has been instrumental in shaping the ideals and aspirations of its members. These ideals and aspirations range from an emphasis on the values of chivalry and selflessness to a commitment to the principles of individual liberty and social harmony.

In addition, the York Rite has long been seen as a potent emblem of both the cohesion and variety that characterize American Freemasonry. Masons come from all walks of life and all corners of the country, and the York Rite has helped to promote a sense of solidarity and shared purpose among them via its adherence to the principles of mutual recognition and collaboration across different Masonic entities.

The York Rite of Freemasonry has been an influential and everlasting force throughout the development of the United States of America. Throughout the course of more than two centuries, the York Rite has been an indispensable component of the social fabric of the United States of America due to its connections to the Founding Fathers as well as its wider cultural and political influence. As such, it is evidence of the ongoing force and continued relevance of Freemasonry in today's world.

York Rite Masonry and the Civil War

The American Civil War was an important turning point in the nation's history, and it had a significant influence on many facets of American culture and society, including the realm of freemasonry. During this turbulent time, the York Rite of Freemasonry played an especially vital role. Many members of the fraternity, on both sides of the fight, took active positions in the war effort, and this resulted in the fraternity having a significant impact.

General Albert Pike, who was a prominent leader of the Scottish Rite in the southern United States, was one of the most notable York Rite Masons who participated in the Civil War. Pike was also a member of the York Rite. Over the course of the war, Pike was a stalwart supporter of the Confederacy and was instrumental in the process of enlisting and organizing Rebel forces. In addition to this, he wrote extensively on the spiritual and moral implications of the war, focusing on the role of chivalry, honor, and sacrifice in the pursuit of a cause that was just.

Another prominent member of the York Rite Masonic order who was active during the American Civil War was General Winfield Scott Hancock, who commanded the Union Army during the conflict. Hancock was a devout Freemason who participated in a number of different Masonic organizations, including the York Rite. On the battlefield, he earned a reputation for his bravery and leadership, and throughout the war, he was instrumental in the outcome of several important engagements, including the Battle of Gettysburg.

Throughout the entirety of the American Civil War, York Rite Masons on both sides of the fight labored to assist their respective armies and further the cause of their respective causes. [Civil War] This frequently entailed providing monetary support, organizing logistical activities, and providing medical care to injured service members.

In addition to this, the York Rite was significant in the larger cultural and political scene of the time period encompassing the American Civil War. A great number of Masonic lodges acted as hubs of political and social activity throughout this time period. Inside these lodges, members of opposing factions of the war engaged in heated arguments and conversations about the pressing issues of the day. The fraternity also played an important part in the reconstruction of the country after the war, with many Masons working to promote reconciliation and healing in the aftermath of the conflict. This was one of the many ways in which the fraternity contributed to the healing and restoration of the nation.

In conclusion, the York Rite of Freemasonry had a significant role in the age of the Civil War that was both vital and complex. At this tumultuous time in American history, the York Rite was an essential component of American society for a number of reasons, including the fact that its famous members fought on both sides of the conflict and the broader cultural and political impact it had. As so, it serves as a reminder of the everlasting significance and relevance that Freemasonry has had in the process of sculpting the history and culture of the United States.

The Role of Women in the York Rite

Order of the Eastern Star

The origins of the Masonic-affiliated organization known as the Order of the Eastern Star may be traced all the way back to the middle of the 19th century. When compared to typical Masonic lodges, the Order of the Eastern Star is frequently referred to as a "fraternal" organization because it is inclusive of both men and women in its membership. The York Rite of Freemasonry is closely associated with this Order, and many people view this Order as an extension of the beliefs and principles upheld by the York Rite.

It is interesting that the Eastern Star places an emphasis on the part that women play in the Masonic fraternity because of this. Despite the fact that women are not traditionally permitted to join the Masons, the Order of the Eastern Star provides a venue for women to participate in many of the same rituals, symbols, and traditions that are at the heart of the Masonic experience. As a result of this, the Order of the Eastern Star has been instrumental in advancing gender equality and fostering an inclusive environment within the larger Masonic community.

The Order of the Eastern Star is subdivided into a number of chapters, and a Worthy Matron and a Worthy Patron serve as the leaders of each chapter. These leaders are accountable for directing the operations of the chapter and ensuring that its members are adhering to the organization's ideals and principles in order to fulfill their responsibilities. The rituals and ceremonies of the Eastern Star generally involve a broad variety of symbols and metaphors, all of which are aimed to assist members in comprehending and embodying the organization's core beliefs.

The five-pointed star is one of the most significant emblems in the Order of the Eastern Star. This star represents the five women who were instrumental in the founding of the organization: Adah, Ruth, Esther, Martha, and Electa. These ladies are revered for their virtuosity as well as the contributions they made to the annals of Eastern Star history, and they continue to serve as examples of exemplary behavior for current members of the organization.

Furthermore significant is the Eastern Star's commitment to volunteerism and charity causes around the community. Several of the Eastern Star chapters are actively involved in a wide variety of philanthropic activities, such as providing financial assistance to local educational institutions, medical facilities, and other non-profit organizations. In order to have a positive impact on their communities and to assist people who are in need, members of the organization are encouraged to make use of the skills and resources available to them.

In conclusion, the Order of the Eastern Star, which is a part of the York Rite of Freemasonry, is an institution that holds a significant amount of importance and influence. The Eastern Star has played a significant part in the formation of the traditions and ideals that are held by the larger Masonic community. This has been accomplished by offering a platform for women to take part in the Masonic experience, as well as through advocating gender equality and tolerance. The Eastern Star serves as a potent reminder of the significance of service, compassion, and dedication to the greater good through its focus on charitable giving, community work, and the virtues of its heroines.

The Importance of Charity in York Rite Masonry

Charity has always played a major role in Freemasonry, but this is especially true within the York Rite, which was founded on the principle of brotherly love. Masonic entities such as the Royal Arch, Cryptic Masonry, and Knights Templar are included in the York Rite of Freemasonry, which is a collection of Masonic organizations. Each of these organizations places a significant amount of importance on charitable giving and philanthropy, and its members are encouraged to give generously of both their time and their finances in order to assist people who are in need.

The devotion of the York Rite to charitable work stems from the organization's fundamental ideals and values. These core values place an emphasis on the significance of compassion, altruism, and service to the needs of others. Masons may enhance their communities and create a beneficial impact on the world around them, according to the York Rite, which holds the belief that Masons can do this by serving others.

One of the most significant ways in which the York Rite contributes to the advancement of charitable causes is through the operation of a number of charity foundations and organizations. They include the Knights Templar Eye Foundation, which offers medical treatment and research to battle eye illnesses, as well as the York Rite Sovereign College of North America, which helps students pursue higher education by providing scholarships and other forms of financial aid.

In addition to providing financial assistance to the aforementioned charitable organizations, the York Rite encourages the participation of its members in volunteer and community service activities. A significant number of members of the York Rite Masonic Fraternity are very involved in their communities' charitable and non-profit organizations, where they lend their talents and resources to people in need.

In addition, the York Rite places a significant focus on providing financial assistance to Masonic orphans and widows. This is accomplished through a wide range of programs and activities, some of which include monetary aid, educational scholarships, and other forms of support. The York Rite is founded on the principle that it can foster a community that is healthier and more encouraging for all involved if it prioritizes the welfare of its own members and the families of those members.

In conclusion, the York Rite acknowledges that giving to charity is about more than just donating money or resources; it also involves contributing one's time, skills, and expertise to a cause. Members of the York Rite are exhorted to put their one-of-a-kind skills and capabilities to work for the betterment of their local communities and to lend a helping hand to those who are in need.

Charity lies at the heart of what it means to be a York Rite Mason. The York Rite is an organization that encourages its members to have a positive effect on the world around them by placing an emphasis on compassion, service, and altruism in its rituals and ceremonies. Charity isn't just a moral obligation; it's also an essential part of Masonic life, which the York Rite demonstrates in a variety of ways, such as by providing financial assistance to charitable organizations, participating in community service, and looking out for the welfare of fellow Masons and their families.

The York Rite and the Symbolism of the Temple

In York Rite Masonry, the symbolism of the Temple is one of the most important themes. Each of these Masonic bodies, such as the Royal Arch, Cryptic Masonry, and Knights Templar, has its own distinctive interpretation of the symbolism of the Temple, and all of these bodies are included in the York Rite. The York Rite is a collection of Masonic bodies.

In the York Rite, the Temple is meant to represent the human soul. This idea comes from the York Rite. The Masonic journey is a process of self-improvement and personal evolution; just as the Temple was erected one stone at a time, each degree represents a step along the route. In the same way, the Temple was built stone by stone. The Temple is also considered to be a representation of the universe due to the fact that its building exemplifies the balance and consistency that can be found across the cosmos.

The Keystone is considered by many members of the York Rite to be one of the most significant emblems of the Temple. The keystone is the last stone that is set into the arch, and it is regarded as the most significant because it is responsible for maintaining the integrity of the entire structure. The Keystone is a symbol of the completion of the Temple and the restoration of its lost treasures when it is utilized in the Royal Arch degree of the Masonic organization.

In the York Rite, the Ark of the Covenant is considered to be a further significant emblem of the Temple. The Ark is a symbol of God's presence as well as the divine spark that is within each of us. It is believed that the lost knowledge and wisdom of the ancients can be found within the hidden riches of the Temple, which is why the Ark is employed as a symbol of this concept in the Royal Arch degree of the Masonic organization.

In addition, the symbolism of light is given a significant amount of weight in the York Rite. The Masonic journey is a process of progressing from darkness to light, which is symbolic of knowledge, truth, and enlightenment. Light is considered as a metaphor of the journey. Throughout the Cryptic Masonry degrees, the applicant is given a series of symbols and riddles to solve. These symbols and riddles represent the candidate's pursuit for knowledge and the quest for the truth.

In conclusion, the symbolism of the cross is given a significant amount of weight in the York Rite. The cross is widely utilized in the Knights Templar degree because it is seen as a symbol of atonement, redemption, and resurrection. The candidate at this level gets admitted into the order of knighthood and becomes a member of a chivalric order whose primary mission is to defend the Christian religion.

In York Rite Masonry, the symbolism of the Temple is one of the most important themes. The York Rite places a strong emphasis on the value of self-improvement, knowledge, and service to others, and it does so by making use of a number of different symbols, including the Keystone, the Ark of the Covenant, and the cross. Masons who belong to the York Rite can improve themselves as people and help bring about a more enlightened and peaceful world if they study these symbols and find ways to incorporate them into their daily life.

The Esotericism of the York Rite

Alchemy and Hermeticism

Freemasonry's York Rite is well-known for the extensive symbolism it employs and the esoteric lessons it teaches. Alchemy and hermeticism are two of the most well-known esoteric traditions, both of which are frequently investigated within the context of the York Rite. Both of these religions have their origins firmly planted in Western esotericism and are linked to the pursuit of spiritual evolution and enlightenment as fundamental themes in their respective practices.

In the ancient practice of alchemy, base metals were supposedly changed into gold through the process of transmutation. But, alchemy is also a metaphorical method of spiritual change. In this system, the practitioner attempts to transform the "lead" of their base nature into the "gold" of their higher self by transforming alchemy from a literal process into a spiritual one. Alchemy is sometimes employed as a symbol for the process of spiritual transformation that a candidate goes through as they progress through the degrees in the York Rite. This transformation occurs as the candidate travels through the degrees.

The Philosopher's Stone is considered to be one of the most significant alchemical symbols used in the York Rite. It is said that this stone possesses the ability to change less valuable metals into gold, and it is also regarded as a symbol of having attained the highest possible level of spiritual development. The candidate for the Royal Arch degree is supposed to have uncovered the long-lost mysteries of the Temple as well as the Philosopher's Stone during the course of their studies.

Hermeticism is another esoteric tradition that has had a significant impact on the York Rite due to its influence. Hermeticism is a philosophical and spiritual movement that can trace its origins back to the ancient Egyptian god Thoth. Thoth was worshiped in ancient Egypt as the god of wisdom, magic, and writing. Hermeticism was developed from this tradition. Hermeticism is a philosophical school that bases its beliefs on a collection of books called the Hermetica, which are said to have been written by the mythological character Hermes Trismegistus.

The "as above, so below" notion is considered to be one of the most important tenets of the Hermetic school of thought. According to this theory, the microcosm is a reflection of the macrocosm, and the entire cosmos may be understood as a single, interconnected whole. This notion is embodied in the York Rite through the utilization of symbolic rituals and teachings that serve to establish a connection between the individual candidate and the broader cosmos.

The caduceus, which is a representation of the god Mercury, is yet another significant Hermetic symbol that is used in the York Rite. The caduceus is a symbol that represents the power of change as well as the coming together of opposites. It is comprised of two serpents that are coiled around a staff. Candidates for the Knights Templar degree receive an initiation into the order of knighthood as well as a sword and a shield emblazoned with the image of a caduceus as part of their training.

The York Rite of Freemasonry has a long and illustrious history of esotericism and symbolism, much of which is derived from the more ancient traditions of hermeticism and alchemy. The York Rite emphasizes the significance of spiritual development and the interconnectedness of all things through the utilization of a variety of symbols, including the Philosopher's Stone, the caduceus, and the "as above, so below" principle. Masons have the opportunity to develop a more in-depth comprehension of both themselves and the cosmos that surrounds them by delving into the esoteric practices that are part of the York Rite.

The York Rite and the Quest for Knowledge

For a very long time, the York Rite of Freemasonry has been connected with the search for knowledge and the attempt to uncover the truth. The York Rite has always placed a strong emphasis on the significance of education, scholarship, and intellectual inquiry, beginning with its roots in the artisan guilds of the middle ages and continuing into its current form as a fraternal organization.

The York Rite uses its degrees and rituals as one of the primary means through which it encourages individuals to continue their quest for knowledge. The purpose of each degree in the York Rite is to instill essential ethical and philosophical principles in the applicant, as well as to inspire them to pursue additional knowledge and comprehension of the world around them. For instance, the tale of how the Temple of Solomon was rebuilt serves as the basis for the Royal Arch degree in Freemasonry. This degree imparts valuable life lessons about tenacity, persistence, and the pursuit of undiscovered truths.

The York Rite places a strong focus on historical research and scholarship, which is another essential component of its ongoing quest for knowledge. The rich history of Freemasonry and its influence on society are topics that are investigated by a variety of research groups, historical societies, and educational initiatives sponsored by a number of York Rite organisations. Masons are able to contribute to the continual search for knowledge and understanding as well as get a more in-depth grasp of the history and traditions of their fraternity by participating in these activities, which allow them to do so.

The York Rite is especially well-known for its commitment to the preservation of historical relics and documentation. This aspect of the organization's work is particularly noteworthy. There are numerous York Rite bodies, and many of them maintain museums, libraries, and archives that are full of unique items, books, and manuscripts relating to the history of Freemasonry. The preservation of these objects and the provision of access to them for the sake of study and research are two of the many ways in which the York Rite contributes to ensuring that the experience and insight of bygone eras will not be lost to subsequent generations.

In conclusion, the York Rite is an organization that encourages the pursuit of knowledge through its commitment to lifelong learning and individual development. A wide variety of subjects pertaining to Freemasonry, philosophy, religion, and history are presented at the lectures, seminars, and workshops that are sponsored by several York Rite bodies. Masons have the opportunity to increase their knowledge and comprehension of the world around them by participating in these educational programs, which also give them the chance to learn from specialists in their respective professions, explore new ideas and points of view, and more.

The York Rite of Freemasonry has a long history of encouraging individuals to seek knowledge and the pursuit of the truth in their daily lives. Masons are encouraged to seek a better understanding of themselves as well as the world around them by the York Rite, which does this through a series of degrees, rites, educational programs, and historical research. Masons are able to develop as individuals, encouraged to make contributions to society, and safeguard the ideas of the fraternity for future generations if they embrace this quest for knowledge as they take their masonic journey and make it a integral part of their lives.

The York Rite and the Pursuit of Moral and Spiritual Development

The York Rite of Freemasonry has long been associated with the pursuit of moral and spiritual development. At the heart of the York Rite's teachings are lessons and principles that are designed to help Masons lead more virtuous and fulfilling lives, and to develop a deeper understanding of themselves and their place in the world.

One of the key ways in which the York Rite promotes moral and spiritual development is through its degrees and rituals. Each degree within the York Rite is designed to teach the candidate important moral and ethical lessons, and to help them develop a stronger sense of personal responsibility and accountability. The lessons taught within the York Rite are based on ancient wisdom and philosophy, and are intended to provide Masons with a framework for leading a virtuous and fulfilling life.

For example, the Royal Arch degree, which is considered the foundation of the York Rite, teaches important lessons about the importance of perseverance, determination, and the search for truth. The Cryptic degrees, which focus on the hidden mysteries of the craft, teach valuable lessons about the importance of discretion, loyalty, and the pursuit of knowledge. And the Knights Templar degree, which is based on the medieval order of knighthood, teaches important lessons about the virtues of courage, honor, and self-sacrifice.

Another important aspect of the York Rite's pursuit of moral and spiritual development is its emphasis on service and charity. Many York Rite bodies are involved in charitable work, such as supporting local food banks, homeless shelters, and children's hospitals. Through these efforts, Masons are able to put their moral and ethical principles into practice, and to make a positive difference in the lives of others.

The York Rite also places a strong emphasis on personal growth and development. Many York Rite bodies offer educational programs and workshops on a wide range of topics related to personal growth and self-improvement, such as leadership development, time management, and stress reduction. These programs provide Masons with valuable tools and resources to help them overcome challenges and achieve their full potential.

Finally, the York Rite encourages Masons to develop a deeper sense of spirituality and connection to the divine. Many York Rite rituals and ceremonies are designed to help Masons cultivate a deeper sense of reverence and awe for the mysteries of creation, and to develop a stronger sense of their own spiritual identity. Through prayer, meditation, and contemplation, Masons are able to connect with a higher power and to gain a deeper understanding of the divine nature of all things.

The York Rite of Freemasonry is a powerful tool for the pursuit of moral and spiritual development. Through its degrees, rituals, service projects, and educational programs, the York Rite encourages Masons to lead virtuous and fulfilling lives, to serve others, and to cultivate a deeper sense of spiritual connection and identity. By embracing these principles and teachings, Masons are able to grow as individuals, contribute to society, and uphold the principles of the fraternity for future generations.

The York Rite and its Global Reach

Freemasonry Beyond Borders

The York Rite of Freemasonry is an international organization that has made a major contribution to the history and culture of a great number of nations and communities all over the world. The beliefs and tenets of the York Rite have been a source of motivation and inspiration for untold numbers of people throughout the course of history, and the organization's influence may be felt far beyond the boundaries of the United States, where it was initially established.

One of the first examples of the York Rite's global spread can be found in the United Kingdom, where the organization has a lengthy and illustrious history. In this country, the York Rite was founded in 1748. The United Grand Lodge of England, which is the governing body of English Freemasonry, maintains a close relationship with the York Rite organization, and it acknowledges the degrees that are awarded by the York Rite.

The York Rite is another important component of Freemasonry in the country of Canada. There is a Grand Chapter of Royal Arch Masons in the country, as well as a Grand Council of Royal and Select Masters and a Grand Commandery of Knights Templar, both of which function independently of their American counterparts.

The York Rite has a considerable presence in Latin American nations such as Mexico, where it is known as the "Rito York" amongst freemasons and is a popular choice among Masonic groups. Other countries in the region include Brazil, Chile, Colombia, Ecuador, and Peru. In a similar vein, the York Rite is well-respected within the Masonic world in Brazil, where it is represented by a number of Grand Chapters and Grand Councils.

In Europe, Masonic organizations in nations such as France, Spain, and Italy have come around to adopting the York Rite as their ritual of choice. Also, the group has created a substantial presence across the continent of Africa, particularly in nations such as South Africa, Nigeria, and Ghana.

In recent years, the York Rite has established itself in a rising number of nations across Asia, including Japan, Korea, and Taiwan, to name just a few of these new homes for the organization. The doctrines and values of the organization have been well-received in these nations, and as a result, the York Rite has developed into a key component of the Masonic landscape in Asia.

The devotion of the York Rite to worldwide brotherhood and its stress on the significance of Masonic unity have made it feasible for the organization to extend its influence to every corner of the globe. Masons from various nations and walks of life have been able to unite under the common banner of Freemasonry thanks to the efforts of the York Rite, which has been successful in bringing people together despite the fact that different regions of the world have varying languages, cultures, and traditions.

The fact that Freemasonry is still popular and relevant after all these years is, in many respects, a testimonial to the lasting relevance and attraction of the York Rite. In spite of the difficulties that the organization has encountered over the course of its existence, it has managed to persevere and advance throughout the years, motivating successive generations of Masons to uphold the values of brotherhood, compassion, and truth.

It is a monument to the ongoing attraction and relevance of Freemasonry that the York Rite is able to reach members all over the world. The organization's dedication to international brotherhood and Masonic unity has also been a significant factor in its success. Whether in North America, Europe, Asia, or other parts of the world, the York Rite continues to inspire and influence a great number of people all over the world, and the repercussions of its work will definitely be felt for many years to come.

The Future of the York Rite

Challenges and Opportunities

Freemasonry's York Rite is known for its extensive history and long-standing traditions, both of which have withstood the test of time for centuries. But, just like any other organization, it is required to develop and change in order to meet the ever-evolving requirements of its constituents. In this chapter, we will investigate the difficulties and opportunities that the York Rite is currently confronted with, as well as the potential future directions that this ancient institution could take.

The dwindling membership of York Rite is one of the most significant difficulties the organization is now facing. The York Rite is not the only fraternal organization that has experienced this trend in recent years; in fact, many fraternal organizations have observed it. This is due to a number of factors, such as altering societal norms and beliefs, an increase in the demands placed on people's time and attention, and the perception that the York Ritual is no longer relevant to newer generations. Notwithstanding this, it is not necessarily the case that the York Rite will perish because of the decrease in membership. Instead, it affords the organization the chance to reconsider its goals and rethink how it will operate in the years to come.

One possibility that could present itself to the York Rite is to place more emphasis on the organization's fundamental ideals and tenets, such as fraternity, generosity, and the cultivation of moral and spiritual development. By placing an emphasis on these ideals, the York Rite has the ability to attract people who share their beliefs and are looking for a sense of community and purpose in their life. In addition, the York Rite is able to make use of contemporary technologies and social media in order to communicate with a larger audience and involve members of younger generations.

One further option that presents itself to the York Rite is to work together with other fraternal organizations and community groups to advance the pursuit of common objectives and principles. For instance, in order to have a beneficial effect on the neighborhood in which it is located, the York Rite could form partnerships with groups that are dedicated to philanthropic causes, such as food banks or shelters for the homeless. This has the potential to contribute to the York Rite's increased prominence and relevance, while also allowing it to accomplish its objective of fostering fraternity and charitable giving.

In addition to these potential, the York Rite must also overcome the obstacles that it is now facing in order to be successful. The reputation of Freemasonry in general, and the York Rite in particular, as being exclusive and shrouded in secret is one obstacle that must be overcome. Although while the York Rite is not actually a secret society, many people who are not part of the organization get the impression that it is. This perception might be a barrier to acquiring new members, and it can also be a barrier to the efforts being made to work with other groups.

In order to overcome this obstacle, the York Rite might work to enhance its public image and increase the degree to which it is transparent. This can be accomplished via participating in community-based activities, such as events open to the general public and outreach programs, as well as by expanding access to information about the organization. Additionally, the York Rite can actively try to debunk myths and misconceptions about the organization by highlighting its commitment to openness, inclusivity, and diversity. This can be done in tandem with the organization's efforts to disprove myths.

The necessity of the York Rite to adjust to shifting demographics and values is yet another obstacle that it must overcome. To remain relevant in today's increasingly varied and inclusive society, the York Rite needs to adapt in order to keep pace with changing times. Because of this, the organization's customs and rituals might need to be reexamined, and it might also need to place a stronger emphasis on welcoming members from all backgrounds.

In the years to come, the York Rite of Freemasonry will encounter both difficulties and potential opportunities. Yet, the York Rite can continue to prosper and make a positive impact in the lives of its members and the community at large if it places an emphasis on its fundamental beliefs and principles, is prepared to adapt to changing circumstances, and is committed to transparency and diversity.

The York Rite and the Search for Unity in Freemasonry

The York Rite is a subset of Freemasonry that was initially established in the United States but has now spread to a large number of other nations. The Chapter of Royal Arch Masons, the Council of Cryptic Masons, and the Commandery of Knights Templar make up its constituent parts. Despite the fact that each of these groups is independent, they are frequently lumped together under the umbrella term of the York Rite, which places an emphasis on the moral and symbolic teachings of Freemasonry.

The subject of unity is one of the challenges that Freemasonry must face in the modern era. Freemasonry is a worldwide organization that is characterized by its extensive history as well as its many customs. Yet, there are a great number of various jurisdictions and regulating bodies that function independently from one another, which can at times cause friction and misunderstanding.

This obstacle is faced by the York Rite just like every other organization. Alongside the Scottish Rite and the Shrine, the York Rite is often acknowledged as a separate and equal branch of Freemasonry in certain countries. In certain jurisdictions, it is regarded as a subordinate organization to the Grand Lodge, while in others it is not recognized at all.

Notwithstanding these distinctions, the York Rite continues to play a real significant role in Freemasonry and exerts a significant amount of influence in the fraternity as a whole. It continues to draw men who are interested in bettering themselves as well as the communities in which they live because its teachings and practices place an emphasis on the significance of morality, compassion, and personal development.

Inter-jurisdictional cooperation is one of the ways that the York Rite is aiming to create unity within Freemasonry. This is done in a number of different ways. A large number of Grand Lodges and governing bodies are currently collaborating in order to develop common standards and recognize one another's practices and customs. This fosters a spirit of brotherhood and cooperation among members of the York Rite by making it easier for them to travel to other jurisdictions to visit and engage in Masonic activities there.

One more way that the York Rite is working to bring people together is by stressing the significance of having shared beliefs and objectives. Although though the York Rite may be practiced slightly differently in different jurisdictions, the York Rite's fundamental tenets of morality, generosity, and personal development have not changed. The members of the York Rite are able to overcome their differences in practice and develop a sense of togetherness by centering their attention on the principles that they all hold in common.

In conclusion, the York Rite is striving to advance oneness in the world by cultivating a culture based on respect and comprehension. Members of the York Rite are encouraged to approach the possibility of variations in belief, practice, and tradition with an open mind and a readiness to learn from one other. There is the possibility that there will be disparities in these areas. The York Rite is able to establish an atmosphere in which individuals can recognize and appreciate one another's unique qualities while working toward a common goal of unification because of its commitment to fostering a culture of respect and comprehension.

Freemasonry's York Rite is an essential and prominent aspect of the organization, and it plays an active role in fostering unity among its members. By emphasizing common principles and goals, cultivating inter-jurisdictional cooperation, and creating a culture of respect and understanding, the York Rite is contributing to the development of a sense of brotherhood and cooperation that transcends boundaries and jurisdictions. The York Rite will continue to be an essential and significant force for fraternity and unity even as Freemasonry continues its process of development and expansion.

The Legacy of the York Rite

Continuing the Tradition of Building the Temple

The York Rite is a set of Masonic degrees that has a long and illustrious history that dates back to the beginning of the 18th century. It has been an important element of the tradition of Freemasonry and has had a considerable impact on the formation of the organization's values and beliefs during the course of its existence. As part of our investigation into the history of the York Rite, we will investigate its place in the annals of history, as well as the role it played in the evolution of Freemasonry and the impact it continues to have in the modern world.

Historical Significance:

The York Rite was an important contributor to the growth of Freemasonry throughout its history. It is possible to trace its roots all the way back to the beginning of the 18th century, when the first Grand Lodge of England was founded. The old Masonic rites and doctrines that had been handed down from earlier generations of Masons were preserved through the use of something called the York Rite, which was designed as a method for doing so. It was also intended to establish a more structured system of degrees, which would serve to organize and govern the practice of Freemasonry. This was one of the primary goals of the project.

Contribution to the Fraternity of Freemasons:

Freemasonry would not be where it is today without the major contributions made by the York Rite. Its system of degrees offers a complete and integrated approach to Masonic education, embracing both the practical and the philosophical parts of the craft, and it is the primary means by which members advance through the Masonic ranks. Its ceremonies are intended to encourage self-improvement and spiritual development, and its teachings emphasize the significance of morality, generosity, and brotherhood. The York Rite places particular emphasis on the significance of the Temple as a metaphor for the inward trip that each Mason must take. This provides a framework for the investigation of the more profound truths contained within the Masonic traditions.

Ongoing Relevance:

The York Rite maintains its importance in today's world. [Citation needed] [Citation needed] It offers a sense of continuity with the organization's extensive history and traditions, in addition to providing a useful system of degrees for people who seek to expand their knowledge and understanding of Freemasonry. Masons have the opportunity to engage in charitable work, make connections with other Masons from across the world, and contribute in the greater community through various service projects and other activities thanks to the York Rite, which provides these opportunities.

Construction of the Temple:

The concept of constructing the Temple is at the heart of the York Rite's tradition as a fraternal organization. This structure is not only a piece of real estate but also a metaphor for the inward journey that each Mason must take. The Temple is a metaphor for the progression from ignorance to knowledge, from imperfection to perfection, and from darkness to light. The York Rite provides a structure for this trip by providing a system of degrees that assists the Mason in advancing down the path towards self-improvement and spiritual enlightenment. This structure is provided by the York Rite, which provides a framework for this journey.

During the course of more than three hundred years, the York Rite has been an indispensable component of the tradition of Freemasonry. Its degrees provide an approach to Masonic education that is complete and integrative, with an emphasis on the significance of morals, compassion, and fraternity. The concept of constructing the Temple, which is central to the York Rite, serves as a metaphor for the inner journey that a Mason takes toward self-improvement and spiritual development. This metaphor is at the heart of the York Rite's heritage. As we continue to investigate the history of the York Rite, we can see that it maintains its significance in the modern day and has the potential to motivate and direct future generations of Masons in their quest for Masonic knowledge and wisdom. This is something that we can see even as we continue our research into the history of the York Rite.